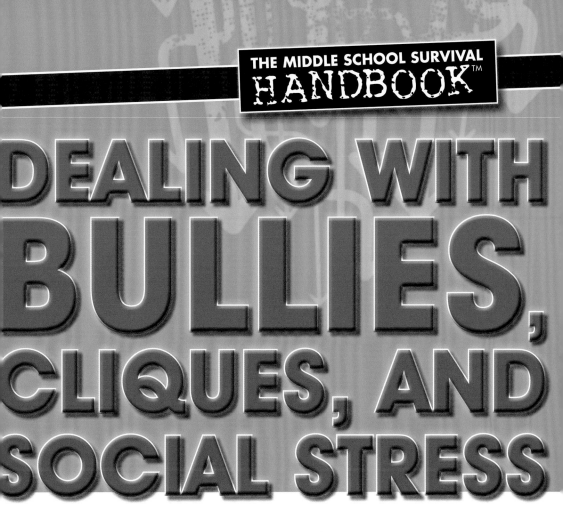

THE MIDDLE SCHOOL SURVIVAL
HANDBOOK™

DEALING WITH BULLIES, CLIQUES, AND SOCIAL STRESS

JENNIFER LANDAU

rosen publishing's
rosen
central®

NEW YORK

Published in 2013 by The Rosen Publishing Group, Inc.
29 East 21st Street, New York, NY 10010

First Edition

Library of Congress Cataloging-in-Publication Data

Landau, Jennifer, 1961–
Dealing with bullies, cliques, and social stress/Jennifer Landau.—1st ed.
p. cm.—(The middle school survival handbook)
Includes bibliographical references and index.
ISBN 978-1-4488-8313-4 (library binding)—
ISBN 978-1-4488-8321-9 (pbk.)—
ISBN 978-1-4488-8322-6 (6-pack)
1. Bullying in schools—Juvenile literature. 2. Bullying—Prevention—Juvenile literature. 3. Psychological abuse—Prevention—Juvenile literature. I. Title.
LB3013.3L354 2013
371.5'8—dc23

2012009244

Manufactured in the United States of America

CPSIA Compliance Information: Batch #W13YA: For further information, contact Rosen Publishing, New York, New York, at 1-800-237-9932.

CONTENTS

INTRODUCTION

There's no doubt about it: when you enter middle school you're entering new territory. In elementary school, you probably had one teacher and one main classroom each year, and spent most of your day with the same group of kids. Everything felt comfortable and familiar, even safe.

In middle school, you have several teachers and different students in each class. You have to learn to navigate the building as you make your way from math to English, and do it all with a lot less supervision and a lot more demands. There are schedules to keep track of and lockers to deal with and students in higher grades that look like they are twice your size.

Maybe the only time you get to see your BFF is at lunch. It could be that your BFF is not even around anymore. People move or go to different schools. People change, too. Perhaps your friend has started hanging out with kids you don't like all that much. Maybe he or she met someone over

Middle school brings many new experiences, such as dealing with lockers and changing classes for each subject. There's a lot more independence, but more pressure, too.

the summer who doesn't seem all that interested in being nice to you.

Once you reach middle school, you're not a little kid anymore, but not a full-fledged teenager, either. "Tween" is a word that's often used to describe students in this age group. Whatever term you use, however, this is a time when you're learning more about the world and about yourself: what thrills you and what bugs you and how to figure it all out without as much input from adults. All this independence is exciting, but it's scary, too. You don't want to be out there alone. You want friends, a sense of belonging. The tension between these two feelings can cause a lot of stress.

If all of this feels overwhelming, take a breath. You don't have to have the answer to every problem figured out right away. Have faith in yourself and in your ability to handle whatever comes your way. As stressful as this time can be, it offers a great opportunity for growth, both academically and socially. By learning certain tips and techniques, you won't just survive middle school, but thrive during these years.

CHAPTER ONE

BULLYING BLUES

It might start with a classmate's nasty zinger about your weight or clothes or hair. That first time, you try to laugh it off or pretend you didn't hear. The same thing happens the next day, though. Soon every day brings another cruel remark or dirty look or even a demand that you do something you know is wrong—or else. You can't figure out why this boy or girl is going after you. You start to feel anxious and depressed and have a hard time focusing on schoolwork. Then the headaches and stomachaches start. You can't sleep at night and wish you could stay home in bed during the day. You are the target of bullying.

Bullying is defined as repeated attacks against someone to hurt him or her. The bully is looking for power, a way to make the other person feel small. Bullies harass and threaten their victims to the point where they can hardly function. There are different types of bullying, including:

Physical bullying—Assaulting someone with kicks, punches, or slaps.
Verbal bullying—Using insults, taunts, and bad language to attack another person.

Verbal bullying is when one person uses taunts, insults, and rude language to attack another person.

Relational aggression—Manipulating the victim's relationships with classmates and friends by gossiping about him or her, spreading rumors, or refusing to let the victim be part of a group. Some refer to this as social bullying. Mean girls fall into this category.
Cyberbullying—Bullying someone using cell phones, computers, or other electronic gadgets.

The added demands and expectations of middle school are hard enough, but these are also the years when bullying peaks. If you learn how to deal with bullies now you'll guard against long-term damage to your relationships and self-esteem.

Why Am I Being Bullied?

If you are being bullied the most important point to remember is that it's not your fault. You did *nothing* to deserve the way you're being treated. Bullies go after someone they perceive as different, which could be based on a bunch of things: your appearance, your family's income, the clubs you belong to, or the friends you do—or don't—have. Kids who are lesbian, gay, bisexual, and transgender (LGBT), or who are thought to be, have a particularly hard time. The Gay, Lesbian, and Straight Education Network (GLSEN) reported in 2009 that nearly nine out of ten LGBT middle and high school students were harassed because of their sexual orientation.

Sadly, kids as young as eleven have committed suicide after being tormented by antigay slurs and other bullying behavior. There's even a term for someone who has been bullied—for whatever reason—to the point where he or she thinks life is not worth living: bullycide.

A lot of people think kids bully because they feel rotten about themselves. Although in some cases that's true—girls who are social bullies, for example, tend to have low self-esteem—many bullies are popular and think highly of themselves. They may even think they have a right to bully you because you don't fit their idea of what's cool. They don't.

Maybe you think you're overreacting. What's the big deal about a snarky comment or two (or three) or a couple of punches on the shoulder when you're headed to your locker? Remember, bullying is not a one-time thing. It's a pattern of bad behavior. Trust your gut about this. If it feels wrong, it *is* wrong.

What a bully might call teasing can be really hard to sort out. Imagine if after every insult he or she says "What? Can't you even take a joke?" Neat trick, huh? Disagree and you might come across as the person with no sense of humor. Agree and you're leaving it up to someone else to decide how you should be treated.

How to Cope When You're Being Bullied

Only you can know how threatened you feel by a person or group of people. If you feel like your physical well-being is at risk, find an adult to talk to immediately. The adult can be a family member, teacher, coach, administrator, or guidance counselor. Just make sure this is someone who will take your concerns seriously. It's true that middle school can be a struggle for all students, but hearing that you should "tough it out" or that "all kids go

Students enter a gymnasium for a school-wide antibullying program. Middle schools have codes of conduct that spell out the consequences if one student bullies another. This type of behavior should never be tolerated.

through this" is of little help. No one should have to put up with being bullied and harassed every day. Schools have codes of conduct that detail what is considered improper behavior, and these policies need to be enforced.

Of course, you don't need to feel like you're in danger to seek out an adult's help. You might have a good relationship with a teacher or guidance counselor and just need a place to vent. Perhaps your school has an on-site social worker who can help you sort things out. If he or she has suggestions on next steps, try to listen without interrupting. That way you'll be able to focus on solutions. If you're worried that others will find out about these conversations, say so. Adults should keep your confidence unless they feel that doing so would compromise your safety.

Perhaps the teacher or guidance counselor can serve as a mediator between you and the person bullying you. He or she might think peer mediation is the right move if the situation is not too extreme. In peer mediation, students who are trained in conflict resolution help their fellow classmates deal with dis-agreements without judging or choosing sides. Although you should never feel forced into doing anything, keep an open mind. There *are* folks out there who have your best interests at heart.

Taking a Stand

Is there ever a time when you can try to deal with a bully directly? Yes, as long as you stay safe and follow some guidelines. An important point to remember is that bullies love to get a reaction out of their targets, so sometimes the best thing to do is nothing. If you don't show the bully you're mad or scared, he or she might decide it's not worth his or her time to hassle you.

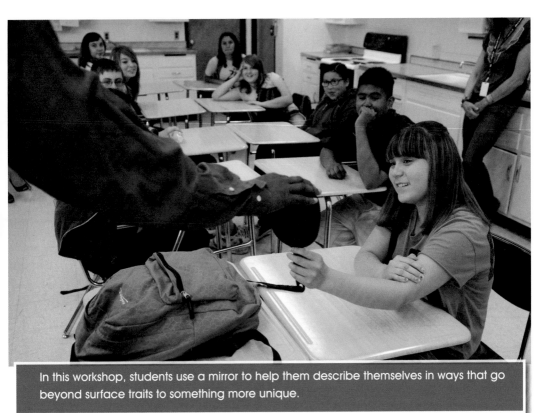

In this workshop, students use a mirror to help them describe themselves in ways that go beyond surface traits to something more unique.

Obviously, this is easier said than done. It's hard to stay quiet and calm when someone's words or actions are getting under your skin. One way to cope? Use positive self-statements. Say to yourself, "I'm smart and kind and don't deserve this," or "I won't let him get to me," or some other phrase that feels right to you. It's also vital to watch your body language, which includes how you stand and use your hands and the expression on your face. When you slump and frown, the bully is going to know his digs did their job. Try to stand tall and keep your face muscles relaxed. The more you practice, the better you'll get at this, so don't give up after the first try.

Should you decide to say something to the bully, keep it short and simple. When he or she insults you say, "That's not true, so stop saying it is" or "Please don't talk to me like that." Do your best to keep your voice steady and maintain eye contact so he

WHAT IF YOU'RE THE BULLY?

It's hard to think about, right? It's not like someone asks, "Who's the bully?" and people all willingly raise their hands. But have you teased a classmate for how he looks or walks or talks? Once? Ten times? How about the girl who just transferred in from another district? Do you give her the cold shoulder every day, having decided she's not worth your time?

Maybe the stress of middle school seems overwhelming and it feels good to lash out at someone else. You might just be copying what you've seen your parents or siblings do at home when they go through a difficult time. Being a bully hurts everyone, though, including the bully. Keep this up and it will affect your ability to form lasting relationships and be successful on the job once you enter the workforce. You'll be more vulnerable to problems with drugs and alcohol, too.

If you're behaving like a bully, talk to an adult about what's causing you to act this way. Perhaps you're overscheduled and need fewer activities and more downtime. It could be your home life is an issue and your parents need to get involved. Whatever the problem is, work on it now so it doesn't overwhelm your life. That work includes trying to make amends to those you've hurt. Taking action will have a positive impact on both you and those you've bullied.

or she knows you're in control and mean business. It's great to have friends or sympathetic classmates around to support you when you're doing this. If at any point you feel unsafe, leave right away and go find an adult.

The Power of the Bystander

If you've ever seen someone being bullied and done nothing to stop it, you're not alone. A study by researchers J. Pepler and W. M. Craig shows that only 13 percent of bystanders try to prevent bullying from taking place. Can you figure out why you didn't step forward? Were you afraid you'd be the bully's next victim? Did you assume there was nothing you could do or that your actions would only make things worse?

It is important to keep the lines of communication open when dealing with difficult issues. These students have gathered during a supervised "circle time" to give themselves a safe space to talk about their concerns, including bullying.

Although it's normal to have these concerns, know that you can make a difference. Refusing to egg bullies on or to even be a witness to their cruel behavior zaps them of energy. They might just see that what they're doing is not only unpopular but also wrong.

You might think that what happens to some other kid is simply not your problem. Not when you have so much else going on in your life. Sadly, bullying affects everyone, including bystanders. Doing nothing could lead to you feeling guilty or down on yourself for not supporting the victim. If this happens often, in time you might become a bit numb to other people's pain, making it hard to form close attachments.

Although you never want to put yourself in danger, you can make it clear that you support the victim and not the bully. Take the student being bullied aside and let him or her know that you're sorry about what's happening. Maybe a group of you can offer to hang out with him or her at lunch or after school. Perhaps talking to a counselor or administrator about how the school can send a strong antibullying message would be a good move. Don't approach the bully directly unless you have other kids around to support you and are 100 percent sure you feel safe. A simple "What you're doing isn't cool" or "You should leave that kid alone" is all you have to say to get your point across. These might seem like small steps, but they'll go a long way toward making your school a safer and happier place for everyone.

CHAPTER TWO

CLIQUE CONTROL

It might not be a word you use often, but it's probably one you know: "clique." So what is a clique, exactly? At its most basic level, a clique is a group of friends who share common interests like sports or computers or fashion. When you're dealing with a new school and new teachers, being a member of a clique can boost your self-esteem. You feel accepted and understood, relieved that there are people to sit with at lunch or talk to in the hallway. These friends help form your identity at a vulnerable time.

Cliques can be tricky, though. Some have rules that are meant to control how you dress or spend your free time. Members of your clique might even try to tell you whom you're allowed to hang out with. Say you have a BFF from elementary school who your clique decides isn't smart or cool enough to be a part of your clique. You swear you're not going to drop this friend, but you don't sit with him or her at lunch anymore. Your afternoons are spent with other members of your clique, so there's no time to catch up then. Pretty soon, he or she is shut out from your life.

It could be *you're* the one who's shut out. You never became part of a clique, or yesterday you were in one, but today you're out. Cliques tend to have an uneven power balance so a few kids

You should strive to be on good terms with all the students at your school, not just those in your clique.

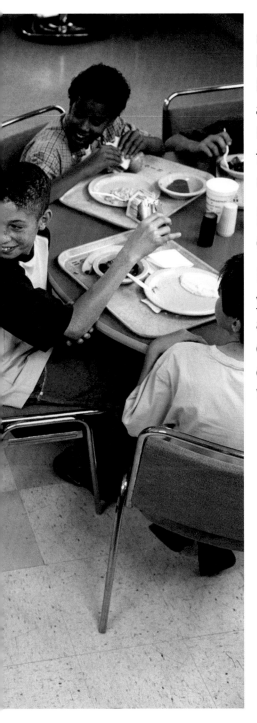

might decide your fate. You don't know why you've been excluded, but you do know that you're angry and sad. Although it's normal to have these feelings, trust that there are steps you can take to make things better.

Does Your Clique Click?

How can you know if a clique you're in is bad for you? First of all, do a gut check. Does hanging out with these kids build you up or tear you down? Want specifics? Well, do you:

- Feel judged all the time? Like being friendly toward the "wrong" people or wearing the "wrong" jeans will lead others in your clique to roll their eyes or make some cutting comment?
- Feel like a fake? Like you're playing a part just to belong?

Middle school is a great time to learn more about other people and the world around you. Kids can have different hobbies and still be friends.

- Feel so exhausted trying to meet the demands of your clique that you have no time for yourself?

If you think the clique still has something to offer you, try to make a change from within. Invite a friend who's considered an outsider to sit with you at lunch. Talk to the boy or girl who's new to your school and encourage others in your clique to do the same. Remember, middle school is a time to learn more about yourself and others. There's no way to do that if you spend all your time with the same group of kids. You should never tolerate bad behavior from others in your clique, either. If someone in the group is acting like a bully, speak up. You might have more of an impact than you think.

Moving On

There may come a point when you decide that it's just not worth it to be part of a clique. You feel drained from trying to keep up with all the rules or worried that you're on the verge of being kicked out. Maybe you were never part of a clique to begin with.

Does that mean you'll be friendless for the rest of middle school? Of course not. All you have to do is open your eyes—and your mind—and you'll see opportunities all around you. Friends don't have to be exact copies of you. In fact, that would be boring. It is nice if you have common interests, though, so think about a club you might want to join or an afterschool activity that appeals to you. Consider reaching out to kids who are in a different grade or go to a different school. The only limits are the ones you put on yourself.

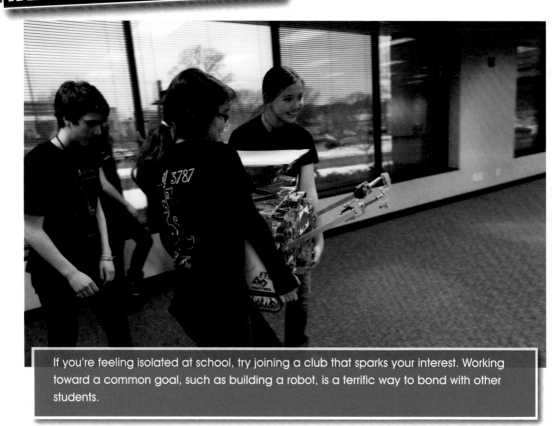

If you're feeling isolated at school, try joining a club that sparks your interest. Working toward a common goal, such as building a robot, is a terrific way to bond with other students.

It might sound silly, but if you want to have friends, *be* one. When you talk to someone, listen to what he or she has to say without judging the comment or worrying about what you'll say next. Smile and make eye contact. Ask about topics that interest your friend and be compassionate when he or she is faced with a problem. It's OK if you don't have a solution. What friends need most is to know that you care.

If you're shy by nature, think of social situations that make you anxious and work through them in private. Perhaps you want to compliment that girl in math class who aced her midterm. Rehearse what you might say ahead of time. You might even practice in front of a mirror to make sure you don't look too tense when you speak. You could pretend you're in a play if that makes you feel less self-conscious. It's OK to be nervous at first. You're trying something new, pushing beyond your comfort level. When you keep practicing and putting yourself out there, your confidence—and your circle of friends—is bound to grow.

Stress Stoppers

When you are dealing with complicated feelings and relationships, your stress levels can soar. You can never eliminate stress from your life, but you can learn to manage it. Knowing that there are things you can do to handle stress will help you feel more in control.

One thing is for sure: you can't handle stress if you don't take care of your body. This means eating right by loading up on fruits, vegetables, grains, and protein and staying away from junk food like soda, candy, or chips. Be sure to get exercise, too, whether it's as part of a team sport or taking a run or a bike ride with a friend or on your own. Exercise releases endorphins, which are chemicals that give your mood a natural lift.

You can't forget how important sleep is to your health, either. Even small problems can feel overwhelming if you're not well rested. You're growing and changing at a fast rate during middle school, and a solid stretch of sleep helps restore both your body and spirit.

If you feel stuck on some negative thought, set a timer for twenty or thirty minutes. Give yourself permission to be as angry or as sad as you need to be for that set amount of time. Try to stay active as you work through the feelings: dance or

Along with eating right and getting enough sleep, exercise can go a long way toward reducing the stress of middle school.

run or take your dog for a walk. When the buzzer sounds, know that it's time to release those bad feelings and figure out a way to move on. That might mean talking to the person who's upset you or to a friend, sibling, or trusted adult. It might mean doing something creative or some type of volunteer work. The more you learn to take pride in your particular gifts and interests, the less likely you are to be affected by someone else's opinion of you.

Shield Yourself

In her book *The Kid's Guide to Working Out Conflicts*, Naomi Drew talks about placing a peace shield and a light shield around

IF YOU'RE SERIOUSLY DEPRESSED

The tips and tricks offered here should help you deal with all that middle school stress. What if your lousy mood doesn't get better, though? You should know the signs of serious depression. Do you feel:

- Angry, sad, or irritable all the time?
- Either unable to get to sleep or too exhausted to pull yourself out of bed?
- Like nothing you do is ever good enough?
- Uninterested in activities that used to bring you joy?

You're not bad or weak for having these feelings. You're simply human, and you should know that help is available. Your school guidance counselor might be able to work with you or suggest someone in the community who can guide you through this difficult time. Don't isolate yourself, as that's likely to lead to a downward spiral.

If you're so depressed that you're contemplating suicide, reach out immediately. Talk to a trusted adult or call a crisis helpline such as the Covenant House Nineline's twenty-four-hour hotline at 1-800-999-9999 (also http://www.NINELINE.org). Remind yourself that there is *always* another solution. Keep pressing forward until you get the relief you need.

you at the start of each day. This isn't an actual shield, but a way to help ward off other people's nasty words or actions.

How does it work? Well, the peace shield comes first. You close your eyes and think of things that make you feel calm and content. Don't stop and judge what images come to mind. Just let the positive feelings wash over you and then picture an invisible shield locking those feelings into place. You can even choose a favorite color for your shield.

Each morning you put your peace shield on so that it's with you throughout the school day. When you start to feel the pain of someone's unkind comment or snub, breathe deeply and remember that your shield is there to protect you. You're less likely to strike back when you have that sense of peace. This will stop a bad situation from taking a turn for the worse.

Once you feel comfortable with the idea of the peace shield, try adding a second shield: the light shield. As its name suggests, this shield sends out a beam of light to surround the person whose negative behavior is bringing you down. Let's say a member of your clique is mad at you for calling him or her out on his snobby ways. Your peace shield keeps you protected while the light shield keeps the other person contained behind a beam of light until he or she is done ranting. What these shields offer are a sense of control and a way to stay focused on something positive when faced with someone else's negativity. Once the storm passes, you'll be in a much better position to figure out what to do next.

MYTHS and Facts

MYTH If you're being bullied, it's because you are weak.

 Targets of bullying might have some difference that makes them vulnerable, but they are not weak. It takes tremendous strength to accept yourself for who you are, especially at a time in life when everyone is trying so hard to fit in.

MYTH Only girls are part of cliques.

Fact Both boys and girls form cliques, but girls in cliques might act more harshly toward those they view as outsiders.

MYTH It's better to be mean to someone online than in person. At least you're not saying it to his or her face.

Fact Bullying is bullying, no matter where it takes place. Also, when you bully someone online the potential audience is much bigger, causing even more hurt.

CHAPTER THREE

MEAN GIRLS

If you're a middle school girl, you want to connect with other girls. You want friends to spend time with and to help you sort through this rush of new feelings you're having, both good and bad. There are all these pressures on you, too. You're supposed to dress right and be popular and get good grades and be great at sports. Add in technology and there's no break from any of this stress, either. In her book *Odd Girl Out*, Rachel Simmons talks about how some girls sleep with their cell phones on their stomachs so they don't miss a text message. They feel bad about themselves if they have three hundred Facebook friends and another girl has five hundred. The need to be included and accepted can become competitive and is a breeding ground for a type of bully known as a "mean girl."

Instead of being physically aggressive, mean girls use relational aggression. They hurt their targets by damaging their relationships with their peers, making the victims feel excluded and alone. Mean girls spread ugly rumors and hurl vicious words and ice girls out—including their friends—when they do something that displeases them. In fact, they often go after their friends, pitting one against another in their attempt to stay on top. Boys can be

Mean girls manipulate relationships to make their victims feel shut out and alone. Pitting one friend against another allows the mean girl to feel better about herself.

aggressive in this way, too, but this behavior seems particularly common among girls.

Although other bullies have decent self-esteem, mean girls, also known as social bullies, typically have a low opinion of themselves. They attack others thinking it will make them feel better about their own lives. There's often jealousy involved in relational aggression, too. The bully is angry because she thinks her victim is prettier or smarter or more talented than she is.

Relational aggression can be hard to spot. A lot of mean girls come off as sweet and well behaved around adults, while underneath they are plotting their next move. It's a nasty game.

Made, Not Born

There's a lot of talk about mean girls in the press. There was even a popular movie with that title a few years back. All this talk might make you think that relational aggression is a normal part of growing up for girls. Have you heard the phrase "boys will be boys" to describe their rough and tumble, physically aggressive behavior? Now it seems like "girls will be girls" equals girls will be mean.

Mean girls are made, though, not born. No girl is hard wired to be mean to her friends and classmates. So what happens? It seems girls are more tuned in to emotions than boys, and they have well-developed memories so slights are not easily forgotten. They talk more than boys, too—remember that need for connection?—and more communication leads to the chance for *mis*communication. That can lead to a lot of hurt feelings.

The media doesn't help, either. Just think of your favorite TV show or series of books. There's bound to be a character that's a bit nasty, and odds are she rarely gets in trouble for it. In fact, her mean girl ways are probably played for laughs. That's not a good model for you or any other middle school girl.

Then there's that push to excel at everything. That's a ton of pressure, and relational aggression gets worse when people are stressed out. You're not allowed to let anyone see you sweat, though. Girls are still supposed to be "sugar and spice and everything nice." You can't be angry or jealous or competitive. Not on the surface, at least. So those feelings go underground and come out in ways that drive a wedge between girls just when they need each other most.

Spotting a Mean Girl

There are different types of mean girls who make their way into most middle schools. It's likely they're in your school, too, so here's what to watch for:

Suzy Snob: This girl is all about labels and money and what famous person you know—or don't. She's great at giving you the once-over and then dismissing you with an eye roll or icy stare if she thinks you don't measure up.

The Gossip Girl: All this girl wants is attention, and she thinks that spreading gossip is her way to get it. She takes bits of information and strings them together like beads, far less worried about the truth than being seen as the go-to girl for juicy dish. The Gossip Girl is so into her game that she might not even realize what she's doing at times. That doesn't make her actions any less damaging.

The Backstabber: This is the girl who pretends to care about your problems but can't wait to use whatever you told her against you. In the morning she's all caring and concerned. By the afternoon, though, she's using what you told her in confidence to mock you. It's the worst sort of betrayal.

The Joker: "Relax. I was just teasing." That's how the Joker tries to get away with her rude nicknames and vicious remarks. She'll harp on one aspect of your looks or habits until you want to scream. Then when you call her on it she'll try to make you seem oversensitive. This is the girl who tries to pass verbal abuse off as humor.

A girl who spreads gossip is desperate for attention. She cares more about looking like she knows the latest dirt than she does about the truth.

Little Ms. Nitpicky: She's a friend, you think. At least that's what she says as she criticizes every little thing about you, all in the name of being helpful. She doesn't like your outfit or your essay or your interest in sports, and she makes her feelings *very* clear. These constant attacks in the name of friendship are wearing down your self-esteem.

Although it might not take away the sting in the moment, it helps to remember that most social bullies feel bad about themselves. They think there's not enough love or attention or self-esteem to go around so they try to add to their pile by stealing from yours. That's a losing strategy in the long run because girls need each other as they head through school and into adulthood. You can't push away those you should be closest to and expect to succeed in life.

How to Cope

What are you to do in the face of all this mean girl madness? As with other types of bullying, remind yourself that you don't deserve to be attacked or excluded. Use the stress busters mentioned earlier to help you keep your cool. Then if a girl says something cruel about your appearance or attitude, try shrugging your shoulders and walking on by. You could also pretend you can't hear her or say "Well, nobody's perfect." She might lose interest in bugging you when she sees that she's not getting under your skin.

To stop gossip, don't be a part of it. Never repeat gossip even if you think it's positive because the message is bound to get

If another girl is spreading gossip about you, ask to talk to her alone. Be clear that what she's doing is not OK, but don't go into attack mode.

mixed up as it makes its way from girl to girl. Should you be the object of gossip, see if you can find the source. There's a good chance she's someone you know, even someone you consider a friend. Ask to talk to her away from other kids. It's OK to be assertive, which means standing up for yourself and asking for what you need, but don't go into attack mode. She might do the same, and this will only make things worse. As always, if you feel like you're in a situation that's frightening or simply too much to handle on your own, get help from a trusted adult.

If you do talk to the other girl, use I-statements, which are sentences that begin with the word "I." This keeps the focus on your feelings and stops her from getting defensive. Tell her "I feel hurt when you say things about me that aren't true" and not "You're spreading lies about me all over the school." You might feel like you're giving the girl an easy out, but the goal is to get her to see your point of view and change her behavior. Be clear about what you need her to do.

Sadly, you might need to let go of this friendship if she's unwilling to hear you out. This will no doubt hurt, but not as much as allowing yourself to be betrayed by someone close to you. Get the hang of using I-statements now and it will become a lifelong skill, one that will better your relationships with teachers and bosses and family members, too.

The Big Picture

If might feel at times like mean girl behavior is here to stay. There are a lot of folks working to make a positive change, though. One organization making a difference is the Kind Campaign, founded by Lauren Parsekian and Molly Thompson, two young women who were bullied during their school years. Parsekian and Thompson travel to schools across the country putting on assemblies and showing their documentary, titled *Finding Kind*, which highlights the negative effects of bullying.

The women told a reporter at TimeForKids.com that the goal of the campaign is to raise awareness about bullying among girls and to give girls the chance to apologize to one another. Parsekian and Thompson have also set up a Web site where girls can share their own stories and make a pledge to be kind. Thompson emphasizes, "[t]his campaign is not about pointing fingers and saying, 'You're a mean girl.' We have all been on both sides of the issue."

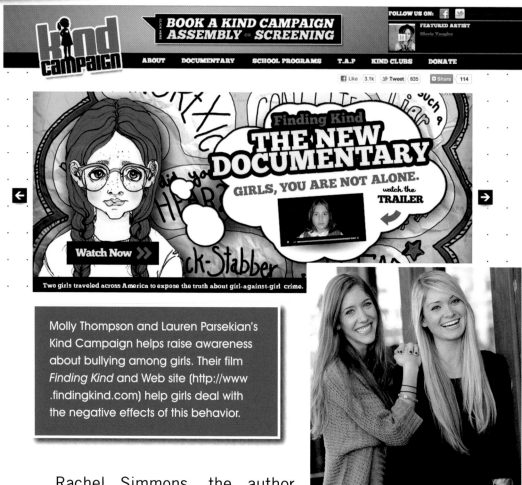

Two girls traveled across America to expose the truth about girl-against-girl crime.

Molly Thompson and Lauren Parsekian's Kind Campaign helps raise awareness about bullying among girls. Their film *Finding Kind* and Web site (http://www.findingkind.com) help girls deal with the negative effects of this behavior.

Rachel Simmons, the author of *Odd Girl Out*, and her business partner began the Girls Leadership Institute. The institute runs evening workshops, weekend retreats, and even a two-week summer camp. According to an article in the *New York Times*, the camp workshops have titles such as "Ending Blame," "Reputations," and "Self-Defeating Habits." There is a "no fat talk day" at the camp, and the girls chant "Food, Good!" as they prepare to eat.

The camp offers a break from the drama of middle school and helps girls get in touch with their fun, playful side. It also helps them solve conflicts by reminding them that they can ask for what they want without acting like either a bully or a wimp. The article in the *New York Times* states Simmons's belief that if girls learn to "resolve tensions with their friends...they will be positioned one day to ask for promotions and raises, and to be treated respectfully by those they love." By learning healthier ways to communicate, these girls are also learning how to maintain both their friendships and their self-esteem.

10 GreAT QUESTIONS
TO ASK A MIDDLE SCHOOL GUIDANCE COUNSELOR

1 My friend seems really stressed out and depressed. Can I do anything to help him?

2 The last time I told a bully to leave this kid alone, the bully threatened to beat me up. Isn't it better to just stay quiet?

3 How do I find friends when I don't feel a connection with any of the kids in my classes?

4 Is there any way to be open about my sexual orientation without being bullied?

5 How do I end a friendship with someone who's just not treating me nicely anymore?

6 I'm sick of all the drama on social networking sites, but how else can I stay in the loop?

7 How do I get my friends to stop using me to pass messages back and forth when they're not talking to each other?

8 If I tell my parents I'm being cyberbullied, I'm afraid they'll take my laptop and cell phone away. Isn't it better to just put up with the bullying?

9 My friends just tossed me aside and won't tell me why. How do I get them to open up and give me another chance?

10 There's gossip going around that I know is a lie. Is it my job to set things straight?

CHAPTER FOUR

CYBERBULLYING

Y ou probably can't imagine life without your laptop, smartphone, and whatever gaming device you love most. Facebook, Formspring, Twitter, and other social networking services sure help you stay in the loop. So do all those e-mails and texts you send every month. According to a poll by the Nielsen Company, young people between the ages of thirteen and seventeen sent on average more than three thousand texts per month in 2010. All this technology can be a great way to stay connected. It can also be a source of a lot of heartache in the form of cyberbullying, which is using cell phones, computers, and other devices to bully someone.

Take the case of Jamey Rodemeyer, a student from Buffalo, New York, who committed suicide after being cyberbullied for more than a year. Jamey was gay and used the Internet to feel connected to the larger LGBT community. According to an article in the *New York Times*, Jamey even posted a video as part of the It Gets Better Project, a Web site where adults try to reassure kids that life as a LGBT person will improve as they get older. "Love yourself and you're set," he said.

Tragically, Jamey wasn't set. He was harassed and humiliated by kids on Formspring, a Web site where you're allowed

Alyssa Rodemeyer gives an emotional speech about her brother Jamey, who committed suicide at the age of fourteen after being cyberbullied for more than a year.

to post anonymously, which means no one knows your identity. The *New York Times* article reports that someone on Formspring posted "JAMIE IS STUPID, GAY, FAT ANND [sic] UGLY. HE MUST DIE!" Although Jamey seems to have been harassed mostly because of his sexual orientation, young people are singled out for repeated abuse for many reasons, including how they look, dress, or speak, or even because they receive special education services. Most kids who are cyberbullied are bullied face-to-face as well, but not having to look at the person you're attacking makes it easier for bullies to be both bolder and crueler.

Many Ways to Be Mean

There are many ways to cyberbully. Along with posting nasty comments on a site like Formspring, Facebook, or Twitter, or a blogging platform like Tumblr, cyberbullies also do things such as the following:

- Spread lies and rumors about someone through a text or e-mail
- Post or forward private information or photos without permission

Amy Boston and her parents sued two classmates after they created a phony Facebook page for her that made it appear as if Amy was racist, sexually active, and using drugs.

- Use someone's password without permission
- Send viruses, spyware, or hacking programs to destroy the victim's hard drive
- Pretend to be the victim and then post something outrageous in a chat room, inviting all kinds of mean comments in return
- Insult another person when playing an interactive game on a device like Xbox or PlayStation
- Ignore someone altogether by refusing to answer a text, e-mail, or other attempt to communicate electronically

In 2010, the Cyberbullying Research Center conducted a survey of 4,400 students between the ages of eleven and eighteen. Of those surveyed, 20 percent said they had been a victim of cyberbullying at some point in their lives, while about the same number said they had cyberbullied others. Ten percent of the students said they had been both a victim and a bully, which shows what a destructive cycle cyberbullying can set up.

As with kids who are bullied in other ways, those who are cyberbullied feel angry, sad, and frustrated. On its Web site, the Cyberbullying Research Center quotes one victim of these attacks: "It makes me hurt both physically and mentally. It scares me and takes away all my confidence. It makes me feel sick and worthless." Kids who are cyberbullied can have trouble with their schoolwork and might be so upset about how they're being treated that they lose interest in socializing altogether. Depression and anxiety can also become a problem.

There's been a lot in the press about cyberbullying leading to suicide, like with Jamey Rodemeyer and other well-known cases. It's probably impossible to pinpoint a single cause for a person committing suicide—several of these kids had issues with depression and some were on psychiatric medication—but reading hateful comments or getting sent a stream of cruel texts certainly adds fuel to the fire.

Parry Aftab, an expert in cyberbullying, thinks that young people who take part in this type of bullying are getting more mean-spirited. She told a reporter at USNews.com that cyberbullies set up fake profiles for kids they want to attack and then get into arguments with dangerous people, leading to real-life fights. "We're going to have real gangs—the Bloods, the Crips—targeted by the 13-year-old nerds who want to hurt a kid they don't like."

Why Do Kids Cyberbully?

A student who cyberbullies might feel angry because he thinks he's been snubbed or is jealous of the attention another student is getting. This kid might be the type who gets frustrated easily or has a hard time following rules. Add in boredom, problems

NETIQUETTE

Netiquette refers to the proper manners to use when communicating on the Internet. This includes things like never pretending to be someone else, respecting other people's privacy by not posting photos or other information without permission, and crediting sources for material you use in papers or reports. If you're gaming, don't use crude language or make fun of someone who lost. To protect yourself, don't ever give out your address, Social Security number, or other personal information, like site-specific passwords.

A great rule of thumb is that you shouldn't do anything online that you wouldn't do in real life. It's tempting to keep typing away, venting about your BFF or teachers, but while you might feel better for a minute, the negative affects could last a long time. How many people will end up seeing that e-mail or Facebook post? What would your friend or parents think? Would you dare say the same thing to someone's face? If you feel like you're about to burst with anger, step away from the computer and try the stress stoppers listed earlier. Find someone sympathetic to talk to: a parent, sibling, or school counselor. Then you can have a productive conversation with the person whose behavior is bugging you.

with impulse control, and the fact that cyberbullies are less likely to get caught, and you can see how explosive this type of bullying can become.

In the book *Cyber Bullying: Bullying in the Digital Age* by Robin M. Kowalski, Susan P. Limber, and Patricia W. Agatston, cyberbullying expert Parry Aftab lists the five major cyberbullies she's seen in her years of research:

The Power-Hungry Cyberbullies: These young people are like schoolyard bullies for the electronic age. They threaten and intimidate others to show that they are in charge and love having an audience watch them do it.

Revenge of the Nerds: At the start, these folks are just trying to defend themselves against real-life bullying. Soon, though, they begin to enjoy taking part in cyberbullying.

Vengeful Angels: Vengeful angels think of themselves as the good guys—or gals—standing up for themselves and others by outbullying the bullies.

Mean Girls: Being a cyberbully is yet another tactic for the mean girl. For her it's all about making sure she ends up at the top of the social heap.

Inadvertent Cyberbullies: An inadvertent cyberbully hurts others by accident, not design. It's his or her carelessness that leads to trouble.

Given all the reasons why students cyberbully and the number of ways to attack a target, there is no "one size fits all" approach to the issue. That doesn't mean there is nothing you can do. Read on for ways to tackle this tough problem!

Staying Safe

One of the first things you can do to protect yourself from cyberbullies is to pay attention to those netiquette rules. Guard your privacy settings. Don't start online fights. If people try to start fights with you, ignore them if you can and block them if you have to. Be cautious about whom you talk to in a chat room. You should be careful even with your friends. If a friend asks to borrow your cell phone, make sure there are no texts or pictures on it that you don't want shared. It all comes down to having respect for both yourself and others. This will help cut down on bullying both online and in the hallways of your school.

You shouldn't respond to rude or threatening e-mails, texts, or posts. Don't delete them, either. Make copies because they are evidence and should be treated that way. It's important to talk to your parents or another trusted adult about being cyberbullied. They can help you sort through your feelings and figure out what to do next. That might mean contacting the service provider (or a school administrator if you think a school computer is the source) to see what actions they can take. If the behavior is extreme enough, it might mean contacting the police. All this is scary, but remember that you've done nothing wrong and that you deserve to be protected.

You should know that there are many people working to take a stand against bullying, including cyberbullying. In September 2011, Education Secretary Arne Duncan presided over the second annual Bullying Prevention Summit, a two-day event held in Washington, D.C. The summit brought government agencies, national organizations, parents, teachers, and students together to discuss the steps that have been taken to combat bullying and how to build on that progress going forward. In a press release, Secretary Duncan emphasized the importance of teamwork when trying to tackle an issue as tough as bullying. "None of us can confront this alone," he said. "When we stand together we can address bullying and fight the hatred, bigotry, and fear that divide us. Our children deserve a chance. We must support them."

There are laws and policies in place to protect you, as well. Although there is no federal law against cyberbullying at present, most states have laws against bullying, and many of those laws include electronic harassment. School policies spell out what behaviors are considered bullying and what actions the school must take in response. Unfortunately, most of these policies don't cover off-campus bullying, and a lot of cyberbullying does occur away from school.

Students at Walker Middle School in Florida sign an antibullying pledge as part of a program that encourages bystanders to take part in the fight against bullying.

No law or policy can guarantee that you will go through middle school without being bullied or shut out from a clique, but they are there as an important safeguard. It's equally important to take care of yourself, your friends, and your classmates. Stay open to new people and experiences. Figure out what triggers your anger and anxiety, and use the strategies you've learned to help you cope. Be proud of what makes you unique. If you are passionate about singing or science, explore that passion and find others who feel the same way. Self-confidence comes from embracing everything that makes you special, even your flaws. In doing so, you will develop the inner strength to carry you through middle school and far beyond.

bigotry Refusing to accept someone who holds different opinions from oneself.

conflict resolution Skills and strategies used to resolve issues between two or more people.

cyberbullying Using cell phones, e-mail, social networking, or other technology to bully someone.

depression A feeling of extreme sadness or gloom that lasts more than a few days.

excluded Kept out or shut out from an event or activity.

frustrated Feeling angry and annoyed at not being able to achieve a goal.

harassment The creation of an uncomfortable or hostile situation through words or actions.

humiliated Feeling deeply embarrassed or ashamed.

inadvertent Unintentional or accidental.

intimidate To frighten a person into acting a certain way.

isolate To set someone or something apart from a group.

netiquette The proper manners to use when communicating on the Internet.

outrageous Extremely shocking or offensive.

permission The right or authority to do something.

productive Able to get something accomplished or achieved.

relational aggression Any behavior that is intended to harm someone by affecting his or her relationships with other people.

safeguard Something that serves to protect or defend people or objects.

self-esteem The degree to which you value yourself and your achievements. People with high self-esteem believe they are worthy of being treated with kindness and respect.

sexual orientation A pattern of emotional, romantic, or sexual attraction toward members of the same, opposite, or both sexes.

spyware Harmful software that is used to gather information about a person without his or her knowledge. Spyware collects data on the user's Internet habits, passwords, and other private information.

techniques Methods used to accomplish something.

vulnerable Unprotected or open to attack.

Bullying Canada
471 Smythe Street
P.O. Box 27009
Fredericton, NB E3B 9M1
Canada
(800) 409-3036
Web site: http://www.bullyingcanada.ca
Bullying Canada provides resources for targets of bullying,
   including a chat room, the *Youth Voices* newsletter, and
   myths and facts about different types of bullying.

The Child Mind Institute
445 Park Avenue
New York, NY 10022
(212) 308-3118
Web site: http://www.childmind.org
The Child Mind Institute helps families dealing with mental
   health issues and offers a wide range of resources on
   bullying.

Gay, Lesbian, and Straight Education Network (GLSEN)
90 Broad Street, 2nd Floor
New York, NY 10004
(212) 727-0135
Web site: http://www.glsen.org
The Gay, Lesbian, and Straight Education Network offers
   information about how to protect LGBT students

from bullying. A list of thirty-five GLSEN chapters is provided.

Girls Leadership Institute
1316 Sixty-seventh Street
Emeryville, CA 94608
(866) 744-9102
Web site: http://www.girlsleadershipinstitute.org
The Girls Leadership Institute offers camps and workshops that teach girls how to connect with their emotions and build healthy relationships. The coursework follows girls' developmental needs as they progress from grade school through high school.

Girl Talk
3490 Piedmont Road NE, Suite 1104
Atlanta, GA 30305
Web site: http://www.desiretoinspire.org
Girl Talk is a program that pairs middle school schools with high school girls who serve as mentors. The goal is to help middle school girls build self-esteem, learn the value of community service, and build a mutually beneficial relationship with a mentor.

National Cyber Security Alliance (NCSA)
1010 Vermont Avenue NW, Suite 821
Washington, DC 20005

Web site: http://www.staysafeonline.org
The NCSA provides resources to help people of all ages stay
    safe from cyberbullying or other threats as they take part in
    online culture.

The Ophelia Project
718 Nevada Drive
Erie, PA 16505
(814) 456-5437
Web site: http://www.opheliaproject.org
The Ophelia Project provides tools, strategies, and solutions for
    those dealing with nonphysical forms of aggression, such as
    relational aggression.

Pacer's National Bullying Prevention Center
8161 Normandale Boulevard
Bloomington, MN 55437
(952) 838-9000
Web site: http://www.pacer.org/bullying
Pacer's National Bullying Prevention Center offers many
    resources to help prevent bullying, including downloads,
    videos, and classroom toolkits.

Safe and Caring Schools and Communities
Barnett House, Suite 427
11010 142 Street
Edmonton, AB T5N 2R1

Canada
(780) 822-1500
Web site: http://www.sacsc.ca
Safe and Caring Schools and Communities is a not-for-profit
    organization dedicated to violence prevention and character
    education for children and youth.

Web Sites

Due to the changing nature of Internet links, Rosen Publishing
has developed an online list of Web sites related to the subject
of this book. This site is updated regularly. Please use this link
to access the list:

http://www.rosenlinks.com/MSSH/Deal

Allman, Toney. *Mean Behind the Screen: What You Need to Know About Cyberbullying*. North Mankato, MN: Capstone Press, 2009.

Bloor, Edward. *Tangerine*. New York, NY: Harcourt Children's Books, 2007.

Borgenicht, David, Ben H. Winters, and Robin Epstein. *The Worst-Case Scenario Survival Handbook: Middle School*. San Francisco, CA: Chronicle Books, 2009.

Brown, Lauren. *Girls' Life Ultimate Guide to Surviving Middle School*. New York, NY: Scholastic, 2010.

Butler, Dori Hillestad. *The Truth About Truman School*. Park Ridge, IL: Albert Whitman & Company, 2009.

Cholodenko, Gennifer. *If a Tree Falls at Lunch Period*. Boston, MA: Houghton Mifflin/Sandpiper, 2009.

Criswell, Patti Kelley. *Friends: Making Them & Keeping Them*. Middleton, WI: American Girl Publishing, 2006.

Desetta, Al, and the Educators for Social Responsibility, eds. *The Courage to Be Yourself: True Stories by Teens About Cliques, Conflicts, and Overcoming Peer Pressure*. Minneapolis, MN: Free Spirit Publishing, 2006.

Dunham, Deb. *Tween You & Me: A Preteen Guide to Becoming Your Best Self*. Deadwood, OR: Wyatt-Mackenzie, 2009.

Emerson, Kevin. *Carlos Is Gonna Get It*. New York, NY: Arthur A. Levine Books/Scholastic Books, 2008.

Espeland, Pamela. *Making Choices and Making Friends: The Social Competencies Assets*. Minneapolis, MN: Free Spirit Publishing, 2006.

Fletcher, Ralph. *Spider Boy*. Boston, MA: Houghton Mifflin/ Sandpiper, 2009.

Flynn, Sarah Wassner, ed. *Girls' Life Guide to a Drama-Free Life*. New York, NY: Scholastic, 2010.

Fox, Annie. *Be Confident in Who You Are* (Middle School Confidential). Minneapolis, MN: Free Spirit Publishing, 2008.

Fox, Annie. *Real Friends vs. the Other Kind* (Middle School Confidential). Minneapolis, MN: Free Spirit Publishing, 2008.

Korman, Gordon. *Schooled*. New York, NY: Hyperion Books, 2008.

Krulik, Nancy. *I Survived Middle School: Caught in the Web*. New York, NY: Scholastic Books, 2009.

Krulik, Nancy. *I Survived Middle School: I Heard a Rumor*. New York, NY: Scholastic Books, 2007.

MacEachern, Robyn. *Cyberbullying: Deal with It and Ctrl Alt Delete It*. Toronto, ON, Canada: James Lorimer & Company Ltd., 2011.

Preller, James. *Bystander*. New York, NY: Square Fish, 2011.

Savage, Dan, and Terry Miller. *It Gets Better: Coming Out, Overcoming Bullying, and Creating a Life Worth Living*. New York, NY: Dutton, 2011.

Sprague, Susan. *Coping with Cliques: A Workbook to Help Girls Deal with Gossip, Put-Downs, Bullying, and Other Mean Behavior*. Oakland, CA: Instant Help Books/New Harbinger, 2008.

Vega, Denise. *Access Denied (and Other Eighth Grade Error Messages)*. New York, NY: Little, Brown Books for Young Readers, 2009.

Vega, Denise. *Click Here (To Find Out How I Survived Seventh Grade)*. New York, NY: Little, Brown Books for Young Readers, 2006.

Verdick, Elizabeth, and Pamela Espeland. *Proud to Be You: The Positive Identity Assets*. Minneapolis, MN: Free Spirit Publishing, 2006.

Willard, Nancy E. *Cyber-Safe Kids, Cyber-Savvy Teens: Helping Young People Learn to Use the Internet Safely and Responsibly*. Hoboken, NJ: Jossey-Bass/John Wiley, 2007.

An, Vickie. "Kindness Counts." *TIME for Kids*, October 5, 2011. Retrieved January 15, 2012 (http://www.timeforkids.com/news/kindness-counts/15141).

Brown, David F., and Trudy Knowles. *What Every Middle School Teacher Should Know*. 2nd ed. Portsmouth, NH: Heinemann, 2007.

Bruzzese, Joe. *Parents' Guide to the Middle School Years*. Berkeley, CA: Celestial Arts Publishing, 2009.

Cooper, Scott. *Speak Up and Get Along*. Minneapolis, MN: Free Spirit Publishing, 2005.

Cornwall, Phyllis. *Super Smart Information Strategies: Online Etiquette and Safety*. North Mankato, MN: Cherry Lake Publishing, 2010.

Criswell, Patti Kelley, and Angela Martini. *Stand Up for Yourself and Your Friends*. Middleton, WI: American Girl Publishing, 2009.

Dellasega, Cheryl, and Charisse Nixon. *Girl Wars: 12 Strategies That Will End Female Bullying*. New York, NY: Simon & Schuster, 2003.

Drew, Naomi. *The Kids' Guide to Working Out Conflicts*. Minneapolis, MN: Free Spirit Publishing, 2004.

Farrell, Juliana, Beth Mayall, and Megan Howard. *Middle School: The Real Deal*. Rev. ed. New York, NY: HarperCollins Publishers, 2007.

Gumm, Merry L. *Help! I'm in Middle School...How Will I Survive?* Douglas, KS: NSR Publications, 2005.

Hartley-Brewer, Elizabeth. *Talking to Tweens: Getting It Right Before It Gets Rocky with Your 8-12-Year Old*. New York, NY: Da Capo Press, 2005.

Hoffman, Jan. "Girls Uninterrupted." *New York Times*, August 13, 2010. Retrieved January 8, 2012 (http://www.nytimes .com/2010/08/15/fashion/15Girls.html?sq=girls%20 uninterrupted&st=cse&adxnnl=1&scp=1&adxn nlx=1328720129-e033Hdy5YSRuDaXd1x8MVQ).

James, Susan Donaldson. "Gay Buffalo Teen Commits Suicide on Eve of National Bullying Summit." ABCNews.com, September 21, 2011. Retrieved January 12, 2012 (http://abcnews.go.com/Health/gay -buffalo-teen-commits-suicide-eve-national-bullying /story?id=14571861#.T_rYIitWrKM).

Karres, Erica V. Shearin. *Mean Chicks, Cliques, and Dirty Tricks*. 2nd ed. Avon, MA: Adams Media, 2010.

Koebler, Jason. "Cyber Bullying Growing More Malicious, Experts Say." *U.S. News and World Report*, June 3, 2011. Retrieved January 15, 2012 (http://www.usnews.com /education/blogs/high-school-notes/2011/06/03/cyber -bullying-growing-more-malicious-experts-say).

Kowalski, Robin M., Susan P. Limber, and Patricia Agatston. *Cyber Bullying*. Malden, MA: Blackwell Publishing, 2008.

Lohmann, Raychelle Cassada. "Cyberbully Protection." *Psychology Today*, July 30, 2011. Retrieved January 27, 2012 (http://www.psychologytoday.com/blog/teen-angst /201107/cyberbully-protection).

Mosatche, Harriet S. and Karen Unger. *Too Old for This, Too Young for That! Your Survival Guide for the Middle-School Years*. Minneapolis, MN: Free Spirit Publishing, 2005.

Patterson, James, and Chris Tebbetts. *Middle School, The Worst Years of My Life*. New York, NY: Little, Brown, 2011.

Ross, Julie A. *How to Hug a Porcupine: Negotiating the Prickly Points of the Tween Years*. New York, NY: McGraw-Hill, 2008.

Simmons, Rachel. *Odd Girl Out*. Rev. ed. New York, NY: Mariner Books, 2011.

Watkins, Michelle, and Sara Hunt. *A Smart Girl's Guide to Starting Middle School*. Middleton, WI: American Girl Publishing, 2004.

Zimmerman, Bill. *100 Things Guys Need to Know*. Minneapolis, MN: Free Spirit Publishing, 2005.

index

About the Author

Jennifer Landau received her MA in creative writing from New York University and her MST in general and special education from Fordham University. An experienced editor, she has also published both fiction and nonfiction, including *How to Beat Psychological Bullying* and *Jeff Bezos and Amazon*.

In addition to her work as a special education teacher, Landau has taught writing to high school students and senior citizens. She has a particular interest in expanding inclusion opportunities for special education students both at school and in the community and in teaching these students to advocate for themselves as they transition to adulthood. When she is not writing, she enjoys reading across all genres and spending time with her son, who is looking forward to entering middle school.

Photo Credits